The Weight of the World

A Devotional for Women in Times of Doubt, Hardship, & Loss in Your Journey to Conceive

By

Emily Jackson

Emily Jackson

Copyright © 2025 Emily Jackson

All Rights Reserved

ISBN: 979-8-9998089-1-2

Dedication

To my loving husband, Ben, my pillar of strength through every trial. And to my sisters, Kelsey and Haley, and my parents, Randy and Tonya—thank you for your unwavering love, support, and constant belief in me.

Emily Jackson

Acknowledgment

This book would not have been possible without the courage, peace, guidance, and strength I have received from God.

He gave me the courage to speak openly about my journey—one marked by pain, uncertainty, and faith—and to share it in a way that I pray will reach and comfort others walking a similar path. In the midst of one of the most challenging seasons of my life, He brought me peace that sustained me, guidance through His Word and through prayer, and strength that carried me even when I couldn't understand the "why."

Thank you, Lord, for the ways You have changed me, drawn me closer to You, and shown me that even in brokenness, You are faithful.

The Weight of The World

My prayer is that every reader will come to know the unshakable presence of God in their own life and feel His love in their darkest moments.

If you don't yet know the Lord, I invite you to pray this prayer:

Dear Lord,

I acknowledge that I am a sinner in need of Your forgiveness and grace. I believe you died on the cross for my sins and rose again. I invite you into my heart as my Lord and Savior. I commit my life to You and ask for Your guidance each day. Thank you for your unfailing love and the gift of eternal life. In Your holy name, Amen.

Emily Jackson

Table of Contents

Dedication iii

Acknowledgment... iv

About the Author viii

Introduction 1

Part 1: Doubt in Your Faith & God's Plans 6
    Day 1: 8
    Day 2: 14
    Day 3: 17
    Day 4: 20
    Day 5: 23
    Day 6: 26
    Day 7: 30

Part 2: Experiencing Loss 37
    Day 1: 39
    Day 2: 42
    Day 3: 45
    Day 4: 48
    Day 5: 52
    Day 6: 55
    Day 7: 58

Part 3: Finding Strength in God............................... 61
    Day 1: 63
    Day 2: 68

Day 3 71
Day 4 77
Day 5 80
Day 6 83
Day 7 87
Part 4: God Gives Hope in Our Most Difficult Times 90
Day 1 91
Day 2 94
Day 3 98
Day 4 101
Day 5 104
Day 6 107
Day 7 110
Part 5: Moving Forward in God's Light 113
Day 1: 114
Day 2: 117
Conclusion: 120

About the Author

Emily B. Jackson is a first-time author, a woman of deep faith, and a dedicated advocate for women in business. As a dynamic speaker, coach, and accomplished sales professional, she empowers women to lead with confidence and purpose. Emily is also a committed mentor and enthusiastic networker, passionate about creating spaces where women can grow and thrive. She lives in Cincinnati, Ohio, with her husband, Ben, and their beloved Scottish terrier, Eddie.

The Weight of The World

Introduction

I'm Emily Jackson, a child of God, a wife, a sister, and a daughter. I grew up in a loving Christian home where we were very involved in our church & my parents showed me the importance of Christian values, faith in God, and living your life each day for the glory of God. I wish I could say I always heeded their advice, but as many have experienced, I wanted to find my way. This separation from God, unfortunately, meant that I started to lean into worldly ideas such as the importance of women to be wholly independent. I bought into the idea that I needed to be independent financially, and to achieve this, I would need to be entirely absorbed in educational and

Emily Jackson

career success. I would not have the time or need for a family/children. I was also deep down, terrified of ever becoming pregnant due to my lifelong struggle with body dysmorphia & disordered eating. I was consumed by the worldly mindset that essentially labeled mothers as "less than". As you can imagine, this caused issues within my marriage & I constantly prayed for God to guide me and change my heart. Just as God had done many times before, He changed my heart and gave me the desire and determination to have a child. I imagine that the devil was not happy with this Godly victory, thus commenced our struggle to conceive & our subsequent experiences of loss. I want to be candid with you, reader, that my husband and I are still at the "beginning" of our journey to conceive. This has been a year and a half process at the time of writing this devotional. I understand many of you are coming from

The Weight of The World

a place of trying for several years. I've spoken with many women who are or have been in this process for much longer than I. At the same time, though, regardless of the time frame of this experience, it's still a heartbreaking and challenging journey and worth sharing. Through my experiences thus far & conversations with women who have or are experiencing this, I know that there is a need for guidance, comfort, and strength from God during our fertility journeys.

Women bear the weight of the world on their shoulders. Even if you haven't dealt with infertility, we've all dealt with doubt, hardship, and loss in our lives. This devotional is for women looking for somewhere to turn during these times. I hope that God's word will provide you comfort, understanding, patience, and guidance on your journey.

Emily Jackson

Welcome to your 30-day devotional journey to strengthen your relationship with God in times of hardship & loss, feel seen/heard, and ready to keep moving forward, loving yourself as a child of God!

- Part 1: 7 Days of Doubt
- Part 2: 7 Days of Loss
- Part 3: 7 Days of Finding Strength in God
- Part 4: 7 Days of Hope
- Part 5: 2 Days of Moving Forward

How to utilize this devotional: This devotional is meant for daily encouragement & guidance for women dealing with pregnancy loss and/or difficulty trying to conceive. Each week has a different focus on what you may be experiencing in this TTC journey & how God can be your guide, confidant, & strength. Each day will also have a journal entry portion with a thought-provoking question or guide to get you going. Feel free to utilize this journal entry as a daily prayer

The Weight of The World

journal and/or a gratitude journal as well. I provide this journal space in this devotional as I have found it helps me to untangle my complicated thoughts in this journey & stay focused on my relationship with God throughout.

Emily Jackson

Part 1: Doubt in Your Faith & God's Plans

As shared in the introduction to this devotional, I wasn't always someone who desired to have children. From as young as I can remember, I determined that I just wasn't a kid person. I never felt comfortable babysitting & just found children to be scary and irritating! I had also decided that I wasn't the type of person to be a good mother. I wasn't especially nurturing, and with how hard I've always been on myself, I couldn't see motherhood as a possibility for me. I now know where these thoughts came from. Society has women believe that their career and individualism are the most essential & admirable things we can do in our lives. I fell right into that trap

The Weight of The World

and suffered anxiety and confusion for decades because of it. However, through constant prayer, I finally found peace and a change of heart in my desire to be a mother. God (as he had done in other areas of my life) changed my heart & I began my trying to conceive journey!

Emily Jackson

Day 1:

Now the serpent was craftier than any of the wild animals the Lord God had made. He said to the woman, "Did God say, 'You must not eat from any tree in the garden'?"

The woman said to the serpent, "We may eat fruit from the trees in the garden, but God did say, 'You must not eat fruit from the tree that is in the middle of the garden, and you must not touch it, or you will die.'"

"You will not certainly die," the serpent said to the woman. "For God knows that when you eat from it, your eyes will be opened, and you will be like God, knowing good and evil."

When the woman saw that the fruit of the tree was good for food and pleasing to the eye, and also desirable for gaining wisdom, she took some and ate it. She also gave some to her husband, who was with her, and he ate it.

Then the eyes of both of them were opened, and they realized they were naked; so they sewed fig leaves together and made coverings for themselves.

Then the man and his wife heard the sound of the Lord God as he was walking in the garden in the cool of the day, and they hid from the Lord God among the trees of the garden.

But the Lord God called to the man, "Where are you?"

He answered, "I heard you in the garden, and I was afraid because I was naked; so I hid."

And he said, "Who told you that you were naked? Have you eaten from the tree that I commanded you not to eat from?"

Emily Jackson

The man said, "The woman you put here with me— she gave me some fruit from the tree, and I ate it."

Then the Lord God said to the woman, "What is this you have done?"

The woman said, "The serpent deceived me, and I ate." - Genesis 31 13

It is only fitting that we start this devotional in Genesis, where we read of Eve's experience alongside Adam in the Garden of Eden. They had been told not to eat fruit from the tree that was in the middle of the garden & must not touch it or they would die. These are God's words to them. Unfortunately, the serpent in the garden was providing doubt and saying instead that they would not surely die & that in fact if they ate from the tree, they would be like God, knowing good and evil.

Isn't this so much like what women experience from society today? We are coaxed into doubting our capabilities, our purpose, and our strength at every turn. Worldly views had me doubting if I could or wanted to be a mom. In our times of doubt due to societal/worldly opinions, let's keep in mind what Eve experienced in the Garden of Eden. As Eve and Adam ate from the tree that God warned them not to eat from, they suddenly felt shame and noticed they were naked. Living the way society deems can ultimately cause shame, loneliness, and doubt, just as Eve experienced. As you ponder the story of Adam & Eve, think about the doubts you've had in this journey to conceive. Have you doubted God's plan for the future? Have you doubted God's guidance? I know I will often find myself relying on myself and not God during this time, but that is the opposite of what we should be doing. Adam & Eve (as well as ourselves) cannot even imagine the plans that God has for us; we don't need to be all-knowing.

The Weight of The World

Journal Prompt: What is something that you have doubts about today? What can your prayer be to God to ease these doubts?

_____

_____

_____

_____

_____

_____

_____

_____

_____

_____

_____

_____

_____

_____

Emily Jackson

Day 2:

"As Jesus was saying these things, a woman in the crowd called out, 'Blessed is the mother who gave you birth & nursed you. He replied, "Blessed rather are those who hear the word of God & obey it." - Luke 11:27-28

In my struggle to give my future up to God, I was determined to never have children so I could have as much worldly success as possible and as much time to myself as possible. The world told me I deserve it! I'm not saying God thinks I don't deserve time to myself or success in my career, but God does desire that we put Him first above all other things. Success & self-indulgence had become my gods and thus had deteriorated my relationship with Him. I knew that he was tugging on my heart to change my mind, and so I

The Weight of The World

prayed that my doubt would turn into assuredness because of Him. I prayed that I would be able to accept the path of motherhood & experience peace with that decision. Little by little, He answered my prayers and gave me that fierce desire to have a child. As soon as I made that decision, my marriage improved, my stress was lifted, & I was at peace. I had gone all my adult life with this selfish mindset, & He was the only one who could change it. If you are experiencing doubt in different areas of your life, trouble conceiving, moving forward after loss, putting your future in God's hands, I implore you to continue to pray that He will lift these burdens from you. Your only Job is to listen & obey.

Emily Jackson

Journal Prompt: Is God saying something to you right now that you just aren't hearing? Has He in the past? If so, how did you end up listening & obeying?

_____

_____

_____

_____

_____

_____

_____

_____

_____

_____

_____

_____

_____

The Weight of The World

Day 3:

"Now to him who can do immeasurably more than all we ask or imagine, according to his power that is at work with us." - Ephesians 3:20

God can do more than we can even imagine possible in our lives! What are your goals for the future? God has even more in mind for you than you even realize is possible or that you are capable of. There have been so many things in my life that I would never have imagined for myself that God always had in mind for me. I talked about my view on having children and how he changed my heart on the subject. He also changed my heart in the sense that He ensured I didn't have a fear of trying new things.

In the last 5 or so years, I've dove headfirst into a new industry & a role that I never would have thought I could succeed at & I love it! He also helped me get back to being involved with a church family & serving my church every week! I thought I didn't have time for that or wouldn't like it, but I feel so blessed every Sunday when I get to serve God & His people. I was recently rewatching "The Chosen" & I found it striking that God would often get frustrated with his followers for their lack of understanding. Still, He would always forgive them because humankind cannot comprehend the depth of God's plan for us.

I can't wait to see what God has in store for me through this time of loss, sadness, and confusion. I know it will be more than I could have imagined.

The Weight of The World

Journal Prompt: What are your hopes & dreams for your future? Now try to imagine what God has in store & your best dreams not being anywhere close to the magnificence He has waiting for you!

_____

_____

_____

_____

_____

_____

_____

_____

_____

_____

_____

_____

Emily Jackson

Day 4:

"As for God, His way is perfect. The Lord's word is flawless; He shields all who take refuge in Him." - Psalm 18:30

Wow! What a powerful verse! This points to our need to live by God's words and His will. When we have doubts about God or doubts about our future, lean into God's word. He will be our refuge. This is easier said than done, right? Especially when you are in a season of waiting & not knowing what the future holds. Personally, my personality type and the way that I go about every aspect of my life is with assuredness, or as close as I can get to it. I am not a fan of unknowns or "playing things by ear." I have a meticulous need for planning. Of course, when my husband and I decided to go for it and try for a baby, I

The Weight of The World

wanted to be as methodical with the process as possible. You absolutely can have control of some aspects of the conception process, but ultimately, it is not in our hands. This was a struggle for me to come to terms with. Of course, I knew this going in, but I thought (as most of us do) that I wouldn't be the one to have any issues. What is so important and valuable about this verse is the direct mention of the Lord's word. We can follow a doctor's word, an app's word, and our family members' words in our journey to conceive. However, the Lord's word is the only one that matters, as He is the only one who knows our future. When we are planning out our journeys, I encourage you to dive into God's word as your guide. Find some favorite verses and write them down, and post them to remind you each day.

Emily Jackson

Journal Prompt: What aspect of your TTC journey and/or loss could you fall back on the Lord's word? Do you have a favorite verse that guides you?

_____

_____

_____

_____

_____

_____

_____

_____

_____

_____

_____

_____

The Weight of The World

Day 5:

"Good things come to God's servant." - - Samuel 6:27-29

Such a simple statement, but with so much meaning. Living a Christian life is not without trials & I've noticed (as I'm sure many of you have) that when I'm closest to God, that is when the devil comes in to try and turn me around. After two pregnancy losses and a prescription that ended up setting us back at least another 6 months, I felt frustrated and tempted to give up. But I continued to push into my relationship with God. I started writing this devotion, continued serving at my church, & working to build Christian relationships with my church family. As things were going so well with my closeness to God, that is when the devil came for me. But I come back to this verse, and I know that it will all turn out as it should (whatever that may be) as long as I am faithful to God. This is another reminder to give those stresses up to Him. Struggles at work? Difficulties in your marriage or family? Recurring health issues? Give those up to God, serve Him, and good things will come in God's time.

The Weight of The World

Journal Prompt: How are you serving God today?

What more can you do to serve Him in your life?

_____

_____

_____

_____

_____

_____

_____

_____

_____

_____

_____

_____

_____

Emily Jackson

Day 6:

"You are not to do as we do here today, everyone doing as they see fit, since you have not yet reached the resting place and the inheritance the Lord your God is giving you. But you will cross the Jordan and settle in the land the Lord your God is giving you as an inheritance, and he will give you rest from all your enemies around you so that you will live in safety." - Deuteronomy 12:8-10

I put my faith in earthly things and became lost. I didn't know how to move forward & thought I'd only be happy once I had more of something (money, success, education, etc.). All along, I needed to put my faith in God & heavenly/divine things. I think this belief stemmed from a lot of different things in my life, but one of them that I can pinpoint is that I've always

The Weight of The World

had a deep desire to make an impact in my life. I didn't know what that was, but due to worldly influence, I assumed that it had something to do with making a lot of money & having a successful career. Don't get me wrong, I love being in the professional world and very much value my Job, but God has helped me realize that this is not what he meant when giving me that desire to do great things. What he meant was doing great things in the service of His kingdom. So, you may ask, what does that look like? It seems like a close relationship with God, trusting Him in the difficult times, praising Him in the difficult & joyous times, sharing my love for Him. God has a plan for us, our inheritance in His kingdom. What I love about verse 10 is that it ends with a simple mention of giving us rest from all of our enemies around us so that we will live in safety. I see a struggle to conceive and experience pregnancy losses as something the

Emily Jackson

devil has put in my life to pull me away from God's promise.

The Weight of The World

Journal Prompt: What has the enemy/the devil put forth in your life? How have you found your way back to God?

_____

_____

_____

_____

_____

_____

_____

_____

_____

_____

_____

_____

_____

Emily Jackson

Day 7:

"Now Jesus learned that the Pharisees had heard that he was gaining and baptizing more disciples than John, although in fact it was not Jesus who baptized, but his disciples. So he left Judea and went back once more to Galilee. Now he had to go through Samaria. So he came to a town in Samaria called Sychaar, near the plot of ground Jacob had given to his son Joseph. Jacob's well was there, and Jesus, tired as he was from the journey, sat down by the well. It was about noon. When a Samaritan woman came to draw water, Jesus said to her, "Will you give me a drink?"

(His disciples had gone into the town to buy food.) The Samaritan woman said to him, "You are a Jew and I am a Samaritan woman. How can you ask me

for a drink? (For Jews do not associate with Samaritans.)"

Jesus answered her, "If you knew the gift of God and who it is that asks you for a drink, you would have asked him and he would have given you living water."

"Sir," the woman said, "you have nothing to draw with, and the well is deep. Where can you get this living water? Are you greater than our father Jacob, who gave us the well and drank from it himself, as did also his sons and his livestock?"

Jesus answered, "Everyone who drinks this water will be thirsty again, but whoever drinks the water I give them will never thirst. Indeed, the word I give them will become in them a spring of water welling up to eternal life."

The woman said to him, "Sir, give me this water so that I won't get thirsty and have to keep coming here to draw water."

He told her, "Go, call your husband and come back."

"I have no husband," she replied.

Jesus said to her, "You are right when you say you have no husband. The fact is, you have had five husbands, and the man you now have is not your husband. What you have just said is quite true."

"Sir," the woman said, "I can see that you are a prophet. Our ancestors worshiped on this mountain, but you Jews claim that the place where we must worship is in Jerusalem."

"Woman," Jesus replied, "believe me, a time is coming when you will worship the Father neither on this mountain nor in Jerusalem. You Samaritans worship what you do not know; we worship what we

do know, for salvation is from the Jews. Yet a time is coming and has now come when the true worshippers will worship the Father in the Spirit and truth, for they are the kind of worshippers the Father seeks. God is spirit, and his worshipers must worship in the Spirit and truth."

The woman said, "I know that Messiah (called Christ) is coming. When he comes, he will explain everything to us."

Then Jesus declared, "I, the one speaking to you-I am he."

Just then, his disciples returned and were surprised to find him talking with a woman.

But no one asked, "What do you want?" or "Why are you talking with her?"

Then, leaving her water jar, the woman went back to the town and said to the people, "Come, see a man who told me everything I ever did. Could this be the Messiah?" They came out of the town and made their way toward him.

I wanted to include the entirety of this story so that you can get a complete picture of a woman struggling with societal expectations and norms. This story is another example of not putting stock in earthly things, but putting your stock in God and God's will. Live for Christ & you will never be thirsty again (spiritually thirsty). This means you won't have confusion & doubt about your life. Living for Christ won't make you wake up every day & want more, more, more of earthly things. You will wake up every day and want more from God's word. When we are struggling to understand why our journey to conceive is not going as we had hoped or planned, think about this Samaritan woman and the conversation she had with Jesus. He assures her of who He is just by knowing

The Weight of The World

about her life. God knows everything about us: past, present, and future. Despite our lack of faith, He still wants to draw us close just like He did for this Samaritan woman. As you move forward in TTC, keep going back to the faith of this woman, and the Lord will guide you. - John 4:1-30

Emily Jackson

Journal Prompt: What comes to mind for you when you hear "living water?"

_____

_____

_____

_____

_____

_____

_____

_____

_____

_____

_____

_____

The Weight of The World

Part 2: Experiencing Loss

To give you an idea of my mindset for this section of the devotional, I wanted to provide you with the backstory of my experience. In November of 2024, I saw those coveted double lines on a pregnancy test! I got so excited and immediately started to plan out my pregnancy timeline. I planned when to tell family and friends, how to tell family & friends, when to have a baby shower, décor for the nursery, all the things! My excitement was unfortunately short-lived as I experienced a miscarriage at 5 weeks (termed a chemical pregnancy). The loss that I felt shattered me. I am not a particularly emotional person most of the time, but this loss was devastating and confusing to me. I became anxious and scared as to what was next in this journey. I truly felt lost in my loss.

The Weight of The World

Day 1:

"Do not be anxious about anything, but in every situation, by prayer and petition, with thanksgiving, present your requests to God. And the peace of God, which transcends all understanding, will guard your hearts and your minds in Christ Jesus."- Philippians 4:6-7

At the end of 2024 and into the beginning of 2025, I dealt with a lot of loss. At the end of 2024, I had two pregnancy losses back-to-back. These were labeled as "chemical pregnancies," which I always felt seemed harsh because they were no less devastating to me. Both times, I got my hopes up and became very excited about the possibility. The emotional toll this took on me was much more than I would have imagined, especially for someone who just a year before was unsure of wanting a child. Through these losses, I realized even more so how much I needed God's peace and guidance. Prayer became my go-to whenever my emotions would erupt (which was often). God gave me peace through this trying time because he helped me realize that the loss I experienced only strengthened my resolve and desire for a child. This would have seemed impossible to me a few years before. He continued to shape me and mold my heart through this time by giving me peace & desire to keep going!

The Weight of The World

Journal Prompt: What can you present to God with thanksgiving today?

_____

_____

_____

_____

_____

_____

_____

_____

_____

_____

_____

_____

Emily Jackson

Day 2:

"Blessed are those who mourn, for they will be comforted." -Verse: Matthew 5:4

Such a simple declaration that can bring us peace in times of loss. Jesus made this declaration to his followers as they were seeking to be healed from both physical and mental ailments. When we experience loss, we immediately seek comfort. Jesus is telling us that it is okay to be in our feels for a bit, to mourn those losses. I would say He is also making a point here to say we aren't alone among each other when we mourn. Doesn't everyone experience times of mourning? And therefore, isn't He saying that He blesses us all and comforts us all? We must seek Him in our times of need and lean on Him. I encourage

The Weight of The World

you to pray, pray, pray if you are feeling lost or alone today. Read God's word to find your comfort.

Emily Jackson

Journal Prompt: What does it mean to you to be blessed? What are you blessed with in your life today?

_____

_____

_____

_____

_____

_____

_____

_____

_____

_____

_____

_____

_____

The Weight of The World

Day 3:

"Come, let us return to the Lord. He has torn us to pieces but will heal us; he has injured us, but he will bind up our wounds." - Hosea 6:1

When you read this scripture, it may seem disheartening at first. Why does God let me be torn to pieces? I've been through so much, isn't it enough? But we need to be broken down to see God's wisdom, hear his word (really listen to it), & live for His glory. My internal battle within myself, causing self-hate, self-doubt, & confusion, has helped lead me back to God. These trials opened my heart to His guidance. Without those trials, I wouldn't have leaned into Him so intensely.

As you experience trials, know that this may be a way for God to have you fully hear Him & be led by Him.

Emily Jackson

Read His word & realize He will heal your mental, emotional, physical, and life wounds.

The Weight of The World

Journal Prompt: When have you felt most torn and broken? Is there a passage of scripture you leaned on during this time?

_____

_____

_____

_____

_____

_____

_____

_____

_____

_____

_____

Emily Jackson

Day 4:

"And a woman was there who had been subject to bleeding for twelve years. She had suffered a great deal under the care of many doctors and had spent all she had, yet instead of getting better, she grew worse. When she heard about Jesus, she came up behind him in the crowd and touched his cloak, because she thought, "If I just touch his clothes, I will be healed." - Mark 5:25-34

Immediately, her bleeding stopped, and she felt in her body that she was freed from her suffering. At once, Jesus realized that power had gone out of him. He turned around in the crowd and asked, "Who touched my clothes?" "You see the people crowding against you," his disciples answered, "and yet you can ask, 'Who touched me?'" But Jesus kept looking around to see who had done it. Then the woman, knowing what had happened to her, came and fell at his feet and, trembling with fear, told him the whole truth. He said to her, "Daughter, your faith has healed you. Go in peace and be freed from your suffering."

This story of a woman who had been bleeding for 12 years and had not been healed by any worldly means is something we all can relate to. There are many times in our lives when worldly things can not heal us. Just the mere touch of Jesus' cloak instantly healed this woman because she had faith in Jesus. What would happen if we honestly lean into God for healing? His healing may not always be in the time or fashion that we expect or anticipate, but God will provide healing if we truly give it up to Him. I know & trust that if I am never able to conceive, God will bring a child into my life in one way or another. Of course, at times I have (& continue to have) moments of doubt and frustration even though I know God's got it. I trust in God's perfect will; He provides what we need. Be confident in that for your own life, in times of loss or feeling lost. Pray for God to have His will in your life.

The Weight of The World

Journal Prompt: What can you pray for God to heal for you today?

_____

_____

_____

_____

_____

_____

_____

_____

_____

_____

_____

_____

Emily Jackson

Day 5:

"Then Job replied to the Lord, "I know that you can do all things; no purpose of yours can be thwarted. You asked, 'Who is this that obscures my plans without knowledge?' Surely I spoke of things I did not understand, things too wonderful for "You said, 'Listen now, and I will speak; I will question you, and you shall answer me." My ears had heard of you, but now my eyes have seen you. Therefore, I despise myself and repent in dust and ashes." - Job 42:1-6

God can do all things! Even when I've experienced periods of loss after loss and things don't seem to improve for quite some time, I find that God not only provides comfort but also helps me move forward. Late 2024 is when I experienced back-to-back pregnancy losses. Then, in early 2025, my grandfather passed away, and one month later, we had to unexpectedly put our dog down that we had had in our lives for 10 years. For 6 months, I had 4 different losses in my life. It was challenging to remain positive and trust in God's plan. But through my church family, God's word, and my time in prayer, I understood that God has a purpose for me. When we have loss, know that God can heal our suffering. He will strengthen you again; only He can do so.

Emily Jackson

Journal Prompt: What can you repent from today to grow your relationship with God? Is there something holding you back?

_____

_____

_____

_____

_____

_____

_____

_____

_____

_____

_____

_____

The Weight of The World

Day 6:

"Brothers and sisters, we do not want you to be uninformed about those who sleep in death so that you do not grieve like the rest of humankind, who have no hope. For we believe that Jesus died and rose again, and so we believe that God will bring with Jesus those who have fallen asleep in him."

- Thessalonians 4:14-14

We do not grieve as humanity grieves, because we have hope in Christ. Christians know that when our loved ones pass, when we pass, we will meet God in heaven. I was blessed to grow up in a Christian household & my grandparents were always a great example to my sisters and me on how to live a Godly life. When my grandfather passed, I recall my grandmother saying that while the situation was challenging for her to lose the love of her life, she took comfort in knowing he is in God's loving arms now. She trusts her faith and knows that my grandpa is in heaven with Christ. This also got me thinking about the lives that I lost in early pregnancy. I'll never get to meet them, but I know they will be waiting to meet me in heaven. Take comfort in Christ and the glory of God as believers who will walk with Him in eternal life.

The Weight of The World

Journal Prompt: Why does this verse say the rest of humankind has no hope? What do you think that means?

_____

_____

_____

_____

_____

_____

_____

_____

_____

_____

_____

_____

Emily Jackson

Day 7:

"You intended to harm me, but God intended it for good to accomplish what is now being done, the saving of many lives." - Genesis 50:20

The typical index in my Bible would have this under surrendering to God. However, this verse makes me think of times of loss in our lives. Things of the world look to harm us; loss of a loved one, struggles with infertility, confusion on next steps, etc. But God is using these struggles to build us back up. Take the time to mourn losses, but know that the change in your life that you experience after this loss will be with God's intention. For me, the miscarriages helped me understand how much I wanted a child and that I was as ready as I was going to be. It also helped me and reminded me that work was (in which I placed a lot of value) valuable in my life, but it shouldn't be taking up priority. Having work be my top priority in my life was more about pride than anything else. I wanted to be viewed as successful in a worldly sense, but I was letting that get in the way of bringing glory to God. As Christians, how do we go about aiding in the "saving of many lives?" Our own lives are saved as Christians, but how do we serve God and save more lives? It, of course, starts with our children and family. I urge you to also look at those around you who are living for the world; those are individuals to introduce to Christ, as is God's intention.

Emily Jackson

Journal Prompt: How has God used your trials for good?

_____

_____

_____

_____

_____

_____

_____

_____

_____

_____

_____

_____

_____

_____

Part 3: Finding Strength in God

I had finally felt like I was mostly back to being myself after my pregnancy loss. We were now in the Christmas season, which is my absolute favorite holiday! I love the amount of baking I get to do for friends and family! My husband and I were still working to conceive and hoping for that ultimate Christmas gift. Our prayers had been answered, and just a bit before Christmas, I saw those two lines on a pregnancy test! I was feeling really positive about it because the line indicating pregnancy was a lot bolder this time. We even took pictures with the positive pregnancy test by the Christmas tree. Again, I started planning all the things that come with a new baby & was really happy. I never expected (none of

Emily Jackson

us do) to experience a second pregnancy loss right after my first. The week before Christmas, I began cramping heavily & went to the emergency room. I had miscarried at 6 weeks (again, deemed a chemical pregnancy). I found myself crying at random, feeling numb and disappointed. I found comfort in my husband, family, & church family. My most outstanding comfort was in God's word & my continued faith in His hand on my life.

The Weight of The World

Day 1:

"Therefore I tell you, do not worry about your life, what you will eat or drink; or about your body, what you will wear. Isn't life more than clothes? Look at the birds of the air; they do not sow or reap or store away in barns, and yet your heavenly Father feeds them. Are you not much more valuable than they? Can any one of you, by worrying, add a single hour to your life? And why do you worry about clothes? See how the flowers of the field grow. They do not labor or spin. Yet I will tell you that not even Solomon in all his splendor was dressed like one of these. If that is how God clothes the grass of the field, which is here today and tomorrow is thrown into the fire, will he not much more clothe you of little faith? So do not worry, saying, "What shall we eat?" or "What shall we drink' or 'What shall we wear?' For the pagans run after all

of these things, and your heavenly Father knows that you need them. But seek first his kingdom and his righteousness, and all these things will be given to you as well. Therefore, do not worry about tomorrow, for tomorrow will worry about itself. Each day has enough trouble of its own." - Matthew 6 25-34

These passages are all about making you aware of what you should put stock in. In times of loss & trials, we are constantly worried about how we will move forward. We worry about the next steps, loneliness, and not having the strength to go on. God is telling us to recognize our value in Him. Do you not see yourself as more valuable to God than the birds in the sky? He ensures they are provided for, and they continue because of Him. Humankind is made in God's image; we are His precious creation. We must seek Him & listen for His guidance. By doing so, He will provide those next steps.

These are words of encouragement, but let me tell you that I've experienced this in my life many times. For as long as I can remember, I've been someone who worries constantly and is always stressed about every little thing. Before God changed my heart to want a child, I prayed that He would take away my constant need for control over everything. I had realized my need for control had caused this continuous anxiety for me. If God could help me give my cares up to Him, I knew I would be less stressed & anxious. And you know what? He did just that! I stopped worrying about every little aspect of life and every conversation & started to pray any time I felt that way. This is something I continue to pray about to this day. God hasn't stopped my worrying altogether, but I know I wouldn't be as grounded as I am today without answered prayers.

The Weight of The World

Journal Prompt: Is there something you are worrying about today that you can give up to God?

_____

_____

_____

_____

_____

_____

_____

_____

_____

_____

_____

_____

_____

_____

Emily Jackson

Day 2:

"In all this rejoice, though now for a little while you may have had to suffer grief in all kinds of trials. These have come so that the proven genuineness of your faith- of greater worth than gold, which perishes even though refined by fire- may result in praise, glory, and honor when Jesus Christ is revealed." 1 Peter 1: 6-7

We, unfortunately, all go through trials. I've shared my trials so far in trying to conceive, and even getting to the point of wanting a child. I also had a trial in a previous relationship where God opened my eyes and my ears to His guidance, letting me know that this person was not the right one for me. I must admit that during this relationship, I did not have a close relationship with God. I had drifted from Him, but I felt confusion in my relationship at that time, and I prayed for clarity and guidance. Seemingly overnight, God put on my heart that I needed to end things. It was the most challenging conversation I had ever had at that time, & I've never been someone who is good at tough discussions. He got me through it and made sure I had support from friends and family during that time. You know what God did after that trial? He placed the man in my life that I am meant to be with. The differences in these relationships were night and day. I was back to attending church, consulting His word, and praying. He stepped in during my tough time, even when I was drifting from Him. I'm so happy that I reached for Him; we must seek Him in our times of need.

Emily Jackson

Journal Prompt: How can you honor God in your daily walk with Him?

_____

_____

_____

_____

_____

_____

_____

_____

_____

_____

_____

_____

_____

_____

The Weight of The World

Day 3

"Then the Lord said to Moses, 'Leave this place, you and the people you brought up out of Egypt, and go up to the land I promised on oath. I will send an angel before you and drive out the Canaanites, Amorites, Hittites, Perizzites, Hivites, and Jebusites. Go up to the land flowing with milk and honey. But I will not go with you, because you are a stiff-necked people and I might destroy you. When the people heard these distressing words, they began to mourn, and no one put on any ornaments. For the Lord had said to Moses, 'Tell the Israelites, 'You are a stiff-necked people if I were to go with you even for a moment. I might destroy you. Now take off your ornaments, and I will decide what to do with you. So, the Israelites stripped off their ornaments at Mount Horeb. Now Moses used to take a tent and pitch it outside the

camp some distance away, calling it the "tent of meeting". Anyone inquiring of the Lord would go to the tent of meeting outside the camp. And whenever Moses went out to the tent, all the people rose and stood at the entrances to their tents, watching Moses until he entered the tent. As Moses went into the tent, the pillar of clouds would come down and stay at the entrance to the tent. They all stood and worshipped, each at the entrance to the tent. The Lord would speak to Moses face to face, as one speaks to a friend. Then Moses would return to the camp, but his young aide Joshua, son of Nun, did not leave the tent. Moses said to the Lord, "You have been telling me, 'Lead these people,' but you have not let me know whom you will send with me. You have said, 'I know you by name and you have found favor with me.' If you are pleased with me, teach me your ways so I may know you and continue to find favor with you.

The Weight of The World

Remember that this nation is your people." The Lord replied, "My Presence will go with you, and I will give you rest." Then Moses said to him, "If your Presence does not go with us, do not send us up from here. How will anyone know that you are pleased with me and with your people unless you go with us? What else will distinguish me and your people from all the other people in the face of the earth?" And the Lord said to Moses, "I will do the very thing you have asked, because I am pleased with you and I know you by name." The Moses said, "Now show me your glory." And the Lord said, "I will cause all my goodness to pass in front of you, and I will proclaim my name, the Lord, in your presence. I will have mercy on whom I have compassion. But," he said, " you cannot seemy face, for no one may see me and live." Then the Lord said, "There is a place near me where you may stand on a rock. When my glory

Emily Jackson

passes by, I will put you in a cleft in the rock and cover you with my hand until I have passed by. Then I will remove my hands and you will see my back, but my face must not be seen." Exodus 33:1-23

This is a little bit longer reading today, but I wanted you to get the complete picture of this story and get a sense of what the people, God, and Moses were feeling. Moses & the Israelites were having doubts about God and whether Moses was the right person to lead them. Moses was questioning the Lord and his lack of presence with him & his people. Haven't we all been there where we ask God's judgment and path for us? Especially in times of loss & trials, we question why God would let this happen. But just as in Moses' situation, God asks us to have faith in Him, even when we don't understand the path or can't see past the right now. I was speaking with a Christian friend the other day about how "stiff-necked" humankind can be. There are so many situations illustrated in the Bible where people are frustratingly stubborn and seemingly stupid, even when they've seen God's miracles work in their lives. When I turned that observation on myself, I have absolutely been the stubborn one. I've chosen to ignore God and His guidance in my life repeatedly. I thought I knew what would be better for me. I assure you, when you lean into God in good times and bad, His plan for your future is so much more than you could imagine. Have faith in the path that God sets before you; only He knows the way!

Emily Jackson

Journal Prompt: Are there aspects of faith you've been "stiff-necked" about?

The Weight of The World

Day 4

"As Jesus was walking beside the Sea of Galilee, he saw two brothers. Simon called Peter and his brother Andrew. They were casting a net into the lake, for they were fishermen. 'Come follow me,' Jesus said. 'And I will send you out to fish for people.' At once, they left their nets and followed him. Going on from there, he saw two other brothers, James, son of Zebedee, and his brother John. They were in a boat with their father Zebedee, preparing their nets. Jesus called them, and immediately they left the boat and their father and followed him." : Matthew 4:18-22

These verses make me think of how we need to be ready and willing to stop our current ways of life and thinking (especially in times of loss) & follow Jesus fully. This is what Simon/Peter, Andrew, John, and many others did because they had faith that Jesus was the Messiah. Did they fully understand what that meant? No, as it is too much for our human comprehension, but that is where faith comes in. When we are suffering, take a step back and ask God for His presence and guidance through this difficult time. When you think about it, what earthly thing can heal a suffering and broken heart? Nothing, only God's love can heal that type of wound.

As I was/am going through the struggle in trying to conceive, I dove back into God's word with daily reading & prayer. God also led me to write this devotional so that He could lead others suffering with loss back to Him. What a beautiful way for God to aid in my healing while reaching others as well! I would have never imagined it.

The Weight of The World

Journal Prompt: What does it take to have this type of faith?

_____

_____

_____

_____

_____

_____

_____

_____

_____

_____

_____

_____

_____

Emily Jackson

Day 5

"For we are co-workers in God's service; you are God's field, God's building." -1 Corinthians 3:9

Wow! This verse gives me strength because it reminds me that I'm not alone; my "co-workers" in Christ are with me. That second part about being "God's field, God's building," to me, that indicates God's presence in our lives and the fact that He has built our love and tends the "field" of our lives. He cares that much about us; we are His! I hope you truly take that in. We are His! When I heard those dreaded words "early miscarriage" for the second time in a row, my building seemed to tumble. But God lifted me with determination, support from my husband & family, and a deeper relationship with Him. This experience also brought me closer to my church

The Weight of The World

family and friends. When I would tell other women of my knowledge, I was shocked by how many (honestly, most) had gone through something similar. I never knew this and instantly felt that I wasn't alone. Finding this out was God's way of reminding me that my co-workers in God's service were with me. It also became apparent in my conversations with other women that they were still so strong in their faith. There is no greater testimony than when you hear of people going through trials and still holding on to their faith.

Emily Jackson

Journal Prompt: Who are your coworkers in God's service in your life?

_____

_____

_____

_____

_____

_____

_____

_____

_____

_____

_____

_____

_____

_____

_____

The Weight of The World

Day 6

"Wait for the Lord, be strong and take heart and wait for the Lord."- Psalm 27:14

I don't know about you, but the word "wait" really resonates with me. I've always found difficulty with waiting. I'm impatient when I'm cooking, impatient while I'm driving, impatient even when I'm walking somewhere! I'm a very task-oriented person in every aspect of my life, and patience just doesn't fit on my to-do list/schedule. When my husband and I first started trying to conceive, of course, we were extremely excited & anxious, for I was quickly impatient. I thought I'd attack this whole trying to conceive thing, just like I do with everything else; put it on my to-do list and quickly check it off! As you've learned, that is not how things have turned out thus

Emily Jackson

far. God has me in a season of waiting. From experience in my personal life, my seasons of waiting have brought me into even better things. I'll give you an example; when the Covid pandemic started, I was working for a large aviation company and had just been in my role for about a year. I had worked very hard to get to this type of success in my career and was really enjoying my work. Unfortunately, the aviation industry was hit hard during the pandemic, and my company cut 20% of its workforce. I was the most recent hire on my team, and so was let go. I was devastated and confused as to why God would put this great Job in front of me only to take it away. It took me four months of unemployment to find another job & I felt worthless, bored, impatient, and irritated! But the industry that God put me in next would be exactly where I could see myself being for the rest of my career. He knew that I needed that season of

The Weight of The World

waiting so that I could reset, slow down, and pivot. I trust that my current season of waiting will have that same positive outcome.

Emily Jackson

Journal Prompt: What do you find difficult about seasons of waiting?

_____

_____

_____

_____

_____

_____

_____

_____

_____

_____

_____

_____

_____

_____

The Weight of The World

Day 7

"And by faith even Sarah, who was past childbearing age, was enabled to bear children because she considered him faithful who had made the promise."- Hebrews 11:11

This story in Hebrews is not just about a woman having a child well past childbearing age. It is all about faith & the strength God gives us to continue to trust Him, even when the world may deem it unreasonable. I am someone who, over the years, has become more confident in myself in so many ways. This reserved, anxious, & shy girl has become a woman who loves helping her customers, giving presentations, and forming relationships. I know that I didn't just one day wake up and become someone who is capable of these things; God has given me the

Emily Jackson

ability to overcome. He has been my ultimate source of strength through everything in my life, good and bad. Sarah believed that God could do impossible things. He can and He will in my life & yours!

The Weight of The World

Journal Prompt: What promises has God made for your life?

_____

_____

_____

_____

_____

_____

_____

_____

_____

_____

_____

_____

_____

_____

Emily Jackson

Part 4: God Gives Hope in Our Most Difficult Times

Following my second loss, as I was healing mentally and preparing to keep moving forward, I had a setback due to medication that likely set our journey back about 6 months. During this setback time, I kept praying for God to take that stress from my shoulders & allow my husband and me to take things day to day. Of course, I have times of frustration and times when I start to worry about the future. God has already shown me that He can do anything in my life. He changed my heart and gave me peace to get started on this journey. I know He has a reason for that, and I'll keep putting my hope in Him!

The Weight of The World

Day 1

"Not only so, but we also rejoice in our sufferings, because we know that suffering produces perseverance. Perseverance, character, & and hope. And hope does not disappoint us, because God has poured out His love into our hearts by the Holy Spirit, whom he has given us." - Romans 5:3-5

Suffering produces perseverance, that's hard for us to hear. We've seen this to be true in so many lives, including our own. Think on the times when you've been at your lowest, did you lean into God harder than ever? Did you become determined to better your situation & actively work towards that? I thoroughly enjoy reading & especially leadership-focused books. Any leadership book will talk about what makes a great leader. Failure & perseverance are almost always mentioned. Why do you think that is? Failure makes us who we are; it teaches us lessons we needed to learn to get better. You can say the same thing about suffering. It helps us become better versions of ourselves by bringing us "back down to earth," so to speak. This suffering produces character & this character leads us to hope. This part of the verse really had me pausing. What is meant by that? To understand this, let's look at the definition of "character". Character is the sum of his/ disposition, thoughts, imitations, desires, and actions. Character gives us hope because we now have a firm grip on who we are & what we want in our lives. We are strong, and the Christians' character is strong in their faith because of suffering & failure. We have hope through our difficult experiences. Hope in God, who pours out his love into our hearts.

The Weight of The World

Journal Prompt: What does character mean to you?

Emily Jackson

Day 2

"The hand of the Lord was on me, and he brought me out by the Spirit of the Lord and set me in the middle of a valley, it was full of bones. He led me back and forth among them, and I saw a great many bones on the floor of the valley, bones that were very dry. He asked me, "Son of man, can these bones live?" I said, "sovereign Lord, you alone know." Then he said to me, "Prophesy to these bones, hear the word of the Lord! This is what the sovereign Lord says to these bones: I will attach tendons to you and make flesh come upon you and cover you with skin. I will put breath in you, and you will come to life. Then you will know that I am Lord." -Ezekiel 37:1-6

In these scriptures, Jesus is saying that he can breathe life into dry bones, and then we will know that

The Weight of The World

He is the Lord. When we look deeper into this scripture, God is helping us to understand the depths of His strength. He is the creator, the giver of life. With Him, anything is possible. This gives me hope in difficult times where all the odds are stacked against me. When I feel hopeless, lost, & confused, God can breathe life into any desperate situation. He is the only one who can pull us from the depths. As I'm writing this, I spent the weekend with family & friends at a family friend's wedding. It was a beautiful ceremony and joyous occasion that I was happy to be a part of. But I found myself feeling sad & hopeless as I looked around and saw all of these couples & women much younger than me with several children. I felt like I was so far from reaching that, or maybe I never would. But then I came home & read God's word & worked on this devotional. It reminded me of

Emily Jackson

the hope God gives us, no matter the situation. He helps us through & brings light to our darkest times.

The Weight of The World

Journal Prompt: Have you gone through a season of dry bones? What does this mean to you? How was God with you in this season?

_____

_____

_____

_____

_____

_____

_____

_____

_____

_____

_____

_____

Emily Jackson

Day 3

"In this you greatly rejoice, though now for a little while you may have had to suffer grief in all kinds of trials. These have come so that your faith of greater worth than gold, which perishes even though refined by fire, may be proved genuine & may result in praise, glory, & honor when Jesus Christ is revealed."- 1 Peter 1:6-7

We've spoken about how trials and suffering mold us, give us character, which then can lead to hope. We are seeing this in 1 Peter as well. What I find most striking is in Verse 7. Our faith has greater worth than gold. With gold, it eventually perishes and loses value even though it has been refined by fire. I am someone who loves gold jewelry. I find it to be elegant and classic. Whether you prefer gold jewelry, silver

The Weight of The World

jewelry, diamonds, etc., you would agree that these items have value or worth to you and maybe even within the world. Is your faith & love of God not more valuable? Does that gold jewelry give you hope and peace for your future? No, I am sure it does not. Your faith in God gives you hope & peace for your future. When we put our trust in God, He continues to "prove" us to bring us to greater understanding, praise, and glory in His name. I want to base my worth on that, not on worldly things. By doing so, I know that God will provide what I am meant to have in my life.

Emily Jackson

Journal Prompt: Describe how you've been refined by fire?

_____

_____

_____

_____

_____

_____

_____

_____

_____

_____

_____

_____

_____

_____

The Weight of The World

Day 4

"At least there is hope for a tree; if it is cut down, it will sprout again, and its new shoots will not fail. It may grow old in the ground & its stump die in the soil, yet at the scent of water it will bed & put forth shoots like a plant". - Job 14:7-9

When we are in challenging moments of grief, it's hard to see the other side. We feel as though we will never come out of our suffering. As this passage in Job states, we will again sprout. Our old selves may die; our trials will die off. True, we are never the same after loss, but as we get the scent of water, the living water that only comes from God, we will grow! I could never have foreseen how I would turn out in adulthood or what my life would be like. God knew the direction I would go. He knew the doubts I would

Emily Jackson

have, the disappointments, the confusion, the loss. But he knew I would grow from all this & sprout fruit from my experiences because I had faith in God and He gave me hope through it all. Let Him give you hope and help you to grow again. Your life story, your journey, is never done through Christ.

The Weight of The World

Journal Prompt: What do these verses bring to mind for you?

_____

_____

_____

_____

_____

_____

_____

_____

_____

_____

_____

_____

_____

Emily Jackson

Day 5

"Remember Lot's Wife! Whoever tries to keep their life will lose it, and whoever loses their life will preserve it." - Luke 17 32-33

When we think of Hope in God, the story of Lot's wife may not be what comes to mind. If you're not familiar with the story, I encourage you to read Genesis 19:1-26. Lot and his wife live in Sodom, where it was a sinful place where the people's hearts were hardened to God. Angels helped Lot flee the city after his home was surrounded by people who were to do him harm. As they were fleeing the town, Lot's wife looked back and instantly became a pillar of salt. This is why God is saying to remember Lot's wife in this passage from Luke chapter 17. We can not put our faith in the material things of this world. If we hope on these

The Weight of The World

things, we are trying to keep our worldly life and essentially place more value on it than our heavenly eternal life through Jesus Christ. By doing so, we are losing not only our earthly life but also our eternal life with Him. Reflect on what this means for your life and keep Lot's wife in the back of your mind as you are experiencing difficult times. She too experiences many hardships in Sodom and throughout her life & yet she let herself focus on those things and not on the offering and hope, safety, and peace that God was providing her. Don't be Lot's wife & place your hope in Him!

Emily Jackson

Journal Prompt: What does the story of Lot's wife mean to you? Have you been looking at the past to guide your future?

Day 6

"The Lord is close to the brokenhearted & saves those who are crushed in spirit." - Psalm 34:18

Psalm has so many excellent references when we need some hope. I love this one because it talks about when we are brokenhearted. The days and weeks after my pregnancy losses, I felt more broken-hearted than I ever had before. It got easier as time went on, but that broken-heartedness turned into frustration, which still stemmed from my sadness. It is in these times that we need to lean on God the most. I encourage you, when you are feeling crushed in spirit, to really focus on prayer. That is something all of us can do, and it's simple and relatively easy. When I pray to God, I not only feel closer to Him, but I also feel unburdened. The act of prayer for me is lifting these worries and sorrows up to Him. I encourage you to take it a step further and get on your knees in prayer. For whatever reason, this helps me to really focus on my conversation with God. It also allows me to take that time to only pray, not multitask while driving or cooking, or doing something else. I would also pose this question to you as you reflect on this verse: Are you living for God daily? Are you diving into/seeking His word each day? Since I've started my Bible reading each morning, I feel strange and lost without it. I need that daily devotion & reading of God's word to ground me for the day and get me in the God-minded mindset. When I do this, even when I do experience stress and trials, I have started my day with God, and He becomes my first thought in that problematic situation. Lift those trials up to God, & he will un-crush your spirit.

The Weight of The World

Journal Prompt: What would you say to someone crushed in spirit?

_____

_____

_____

_____

_____

_____

_____

_____

_____

_____

_____

_____

_____

_____

Emily Jackson

Day 7

"Therefore, as God's chosen people, holy & dearly loved, clothe yourselves with compassion, kindness, humility, gentleness, & patience. Bear with each other & forgive one another if any of you has a grievance against someone, forgive as the Lord forgave you. And over all these virtues put on love, which binds them all together in perfect unity." -Colossians 3 12-14

I like that these verses focus on forgiveness. In trying to conceive, we can become very frustrated, and women often have a feeling of shame—either shame of not being able to get pregnant or shame of pregnancy loss. Diving into the inappropriateness of this societal thought is a deeper conversation, but what I do want to focus on is forgiving ourselves. Not

The Weight of The World

forgiveness for not being able to conceive or carry to term, but forgiving ourselves for doubt in God's abilities & plans for our lives. These verses also mention patience; we must clothe ourselves in patience. Easier said than done, but God requires this of us. Then we must love ourselves, love our bodies that God so artfully created. Our bodies will do what God has meant for each individual body to do. It may not look like what plans we have for our lives; we must trust God's wisdom.

Emily Jackson

Journal Prompt: Is there a time that you've struggled to clothe yourself in patience?

_____

_____

_____

_____

_____

_____

_____

_____

_____

_____

_____

_____

_____

_____

Part 5: Moving Forward in God's Light

As my husband and I continue our journey to conceive and are vehemently hoping for good news any time now, I want to encourage you that through faith, you can have peace & guidance during this time. It's only natural for us mere mortals to have doubts, even with the knowledge of what God's done in our lives in the past. Each time those doubts, times of loss, confusion, loneliness, and lack of understanding creep in, turn to God. Know that only He can guide you through the good and the bad times in your walk with Him.

Emily Jackson

Day 1:

"Brothers and sisters, I do not consider myself yet to have taken hold of it. But one thing I do: Forgetting what is behind and straining toward what is ahead, I press toward the goal to win the prize for which God has called me heavenward in Christ Jesus." - Philippians 3 13-14

Amid the most challenging parts of this journey thus far, I would be lying if I said I never looked back. I wondered if I could have done something different; I had a lot of what-if questions. But if you've ever been in a place where you are asking the what-ifs and dwelling in past difficulties, you know that this changes nothing and prevents your future. God doesn't want us to dwell in the past; our trials have a purpose in that we grow our relationship with God through them and continue to build our faith as we move forward. I am thankful for God pulling me closer to Him and using me as a vessel to help share His word, His grace, His strength, & His love. You are a vessel to share God's glory, too! As Christians, we are all working towards that ultimate future in heaven. In quiet moments, I think about the ones I've lost, and while difficult for me here on earth, I trust that in being with God in heaven, they are more loved than I could have ever imagined.

Emily Jackson

Journal Prompt: What do you keep looking back on that is keeping you from moving forward?

_____

_____

_____

_____

_____

_____

_____

_____

_____

_____

_____

_____

_____

The Weight of The World

Day 2:

"Forget the former things; do not dwell on the past. See, I am doing a new thing! Now it springs up; do you not perceive it? I am making a way in the wilderness and streams in wasteland." - Isaiah 43 18-19

Although this past year has been a tough one for me, my husband, & my family, I have hope in the future because God makes a way in the wilderness. He put this devotion in my heart and has given me the courage to share my experience. Through me, His glory will shine! He is doing a new thing in my life, not just through this book, but in so many other ways. My prayer life is enriched, I read my bible daily, and I continue to get involved with my church family. Open your heart and life to God today & let Him guide your path to show you how to glorify Him even on your worst days. He will save you & save others through you. Forget the former things!

Thank you for taking the time to read my devotional book. I hope that by sharing my story, you don't feel alone in your experiences. If you take away just one thing from this read, I pray that it is a stronger relationship with Christ. You are loved, supported, & cherished in God's name.

The Weight of The World

Journal Prompt: What are some new things that God is doing in your life? What are some new things you can pray for Him to do?

_____

_____

_____

_____

_____

_____

_____

_____

_____

_____

_____

_____

Conclusion:

Thank you for taking the time to not only read this book, but really take it in. I encourage you to continue to reference these verses and start to find additional verses in your Bible to help guide you during your TTC journey. I will be doing the same; my husband and I continue to work towards conceiving, and I'm taking this season to not be so rigid, scheduled, and precise about it. I'm giving this up to God, and as hard as it is for me to feel I don't have a plan, I know that He does. If you are feeling alone in this journey or in experiencing loss, please talk to women in your family, network, and church family. I am confident that you will come to find you are not alone & you will take comfort in your shared experiences and learn from one another. I pray that you build your relationship with God so deeply during this time that He shapes

The Weight of The World

and molds you to prepare you for all of the wonderful

things to come in your life. Have faith in Him, always!

www.ingramcontent.com/pod-product-compliance
Lightning Source LLC
Chambersburg PA
CBHW060515030426
42337CB00015B/1904